Relations of the District of Columbia to the General Government.

Is Washington City the Capital of the United States, or the Capital of the District of Columbia?

The Duty of the Nation toward its Capital.

SPEECH

OF

HON. NORTON P. CHIPMAN,

OF THE

DISTRICT OF COLUMBIA,

IN

THE HOUSE OF REPRESENTATIVES,

FEBRUARY 28, 1874.

WASHINGTON:
GOVERNMENT PRINTING OFFICE.
1874.

SPEECH

OF

HON. NORTON P. CHIPMAN.

The House being in Committee of the Whole on the state of the Union, on the relations of the District of Columbia to the General Government, and the duty of the nation toward its capital.

Mr. CHIPMAN. Mr. Chairman, the difficulty which I have found in tracing the relations of the District of Columbia to the General Government, and the embarrassment I have experienced in ascertaining important facts upon that subject, have induced me to relieve others of the labor which I have been forced to undertake by presenting a succinct history of these relations; and growing out of this subject I have found equal difficulty in determining precisely what has been done by the nation for its capital in the way of improvements of streets, avenues, parks, reservations, and the like, and what has also been done by the local authorities.

It occurred to me that the great public interest now being felt upon this subject would warrant a careful examination into it, and that I might be able to render the House some service in collating the essential facts; and I shall feel amply repaid if I shall be the means of enlarging the vision of any member toward the national capital, or of enlightening a public sentiment which I believe is ready to demand of Congress that the Government shall no longer neglect the pledges of the early fathers to build here a metropolis which shall illustrate the origin, growth, and progress of our civilization.

PRELIMINARY HISTORY.

One of the first important questions which challenged the attention of the Continental Congress at the close of the Revolution was the selection of a permanent seat of Government. Congress was practically on wheels, and had held its sessions at Philadelphia, Baltimore, York, Princeton, Annapolis, Trenton, and New York City. The fathers saw that the permanency of the capital would have much to do with the permanency of the Government itself, and it became, therefore, one of the first questions seriously considered.

When in June, 1783, Congress, sitting at Philadelphia, felt itself insulted by a band of mutineers whom the State authorities could not quell, the subject of possessing territory for a permanent seat of Government, exclusively within Government control, became a practical question, and continued to be discussed until the adoption of the Constitution.

In October, 1784, after full debate, Congress, sitting at Trenton, passed an ordinance creating a commission, with full power to lay out a district on the Delaware River for the Federal city.

The ordinance and the debate form an important link in the history of the location of the capital, and illustrate the enlarged views thus early entertained, and which were subsequently carried out in the final location of the capital on the Potomac River.

The location upon the Delaware seemed not satisfactory, and it was probably owing to that cause that the commissioners never entered upon their duties; but the subject continued to attract public attention, and came before the Continental Congress in various forms.

The debates which took place and the public sentiment which found expression in pamphlets and newspapers show that few questions have excited greater interest or seem to have been regarded as fraught with greater importance to the country.

Some of the ablest men of the time took part in the discussion, and treated the subject as one eminently worthy to arouse the patriotism of the people.

Without suggesting the various considerations of climate, locality, &c., which led to the establishment at the present spot, I need only, for my present purpose, refer to one on which there was general agreement, namely, that the present and future good of the Republic demanded that the location should be remote from any of the great cities then springing up. It was thought impolitic to attach it even to the suburb of a commercial city, or that it should itself become one, and it was therefore resolved to found a new city with reference only to the convenience, safety, and glory of the nation.

It was directly with reference to this fact that a provision was placed in the Constitution withdrawing from the States all legislative control over the district in which the capital might be located, and placing it in the exclusive power of Congress. This exclusive control was regarded as essential to bestow dignity and independence on the Government.

Upon this question Mr. Madison wrote in the Federalist:

> Without it, not only the public authority might be insulted and its proceedings be interrupted with impunity, but a dependence of the members of the General Government on the State comprehending the seat of government, for protection in the exercise of their duty, might bring on the national councils an imputation of awe, or influence equally dishonorable to the Government, and dissatisfactory to the other members of the Confederacy. This consideration has the more weight, as the gradual accumulation of public improvements at the stationary residence of Government would be too great a public pledge to be left in the hands of a single State, and would create so many obstacles to a removal of the Government as still further to abridge its necessary independence.

But without noticing further in this connection the preliminary history, I assert *that the history of the location of the capital, the declarations of its founders, the provisions of the deed of conveyance made by the proprietors of the soil, the contemporaneous acts, the plan of the city, and the legislation of Congress, show a distinct and unmistakable purpose on the part of the United States to build here a Federal city at Federal expense.* I cannot hope, in the limit which I am forced to place on myself on this occasion, to present more than a skeleton of the evidence establishing this proposition.

LOCATION OF THE CAPITAL.

I have alluded to the debates upon the subject as showing the importance attached to it.

Mr. Scott said:

> The future tranquillity and well-being of the United States depend as much on this as any question that ever had or could come before Congress.

Fisher Ames remarked:

> That every principle of pride and honor, and even of patriotism, was involved in it.

No Senator or Member treated the subject except as one of the profoundest importance; and this feeling must be considered when we come to notice what was ultimately done in relation to it.

It must be remembered that our capital city was located in the midst of a virgin forest; it was literally the creation of the Government. No consideration was allowed to stand in the way of making it precisely what the Government desired it should be, and this purpose was reached after that calm deliberation which characterized all the important acts of the early fathers.

There was involved in the very idea of building up a great political and non-commercial city, with the chief view of accommodating the necessities of the Government, the implied pledge that Government would take upon itself the burden of public improvements in that city.

A city deprived of commerce and manufactures is deprived of the means of self-support. The founders could not have been ignorant of the fact that to make the capital what they designed it to be was impossible except under the fostering care of Government.

A city without revenues could not provide those expensive means essential alike to health and comfort.

To build a great city, as was the evident purpose of the founders this should be, without aid of the Government, and without local revenues, was an impossibility. No nation before had ever attempted it, and it is absolutely certain that ours never intended to do so.

Turning to the Old World, we find that all the great cities have been either the creation of the state, or have been fostered and aided by the state, notwithstanding most of them have large commerce, manufactures, and revenues.

I will venture to say that since Washington City became our capital, the government of France has expended not less than $200,000,000 upon the city of Paris. Under the first Napoleon over $20,000,000 were expended on public works. Louis Philippe continued these liberal expenditures, while Louis Napoleon surpassed all his predecessors in his zeal for embellishing their capital city. For the ten years following 1859 the expenditures for public works were limited to 18,000,000 francs annually, of which the State paid 5,000,000. During all this period Paris has had a revenue greatly exceeding the expenditures both of government and the city, and her citizens have not felt the burden of this great outlay; while the citizens of our capital, with a revenue but little more than sufficient to pay its ordinary municipal expenses, may be said to have done almost everything that has been accomplished so far toward the realization of its founders.

The act for establishing a permanent seat of government was approved July 16, 1790. It authorized the President to appoint three commissioners, who should under his direction have power—

> To purchase or accept such quantity of land * * * as the President shall deem proper *for the use of the United States*, and *according to such plans as the President shall approve*, and also to provide suitable buildings for the accommodation of Congress, for the President, and for the public offices of the Government of the United States, the same to be in readiness by the first Monday of December, 1800.

The language, as well as its spirit, shows clearly that the city was founded for the use of the United States. Its plan was to be formed by the United States commissioners, and approved by the President. No interests were consulted except those of the United States, as we shall soon see. The plan of the city finally adopted was in keeping with the enlarged views of its founders, and in direct and absolute violation of every law which should govern in laying out a commercial or business city.

DEED OF CONVEYANCE.

The commissioners entered upon their duties with great zeal, while the watchful eye of President Washington was always upon them.

The present limits of the city were fixed upon, and on the 29th of June, 1791, the deed of conveyance by the original proprietors of the soil was executed.

The deed was made upon certain special trusts, some of which I will notice as important in showing the purpose of the founders. The first one was:

That *all* the said lands are hereby bargained and sold, *or such part thereof as may be thought necessary* or proper, to be laid out, together with other lands within the said limits *for a Federal city*, with such streets, squares, and parcels and lots *as the President of the United States for the time being shall approve.*

Thus the proprietors parted with all the soil for the purpose of building here a Federal city, leaving it exclusively with the President to select from the whole whatever he might deem necessary or desirable for that purpose. No reservation was made in the deed for the benefit of the proprietors, other than that after the President had indicated all the streets, squares, parcels, and lots that he should deem proper for the use of the United States, there should be—

A fair and equal division of the remaining lots, and the United States should pay for its reservations and lots at the rate of twenty-five pounds sterling per acre.

The deed does not provide for the dedication of any public squares, streets, or avenues to the public use, but the absolute fee-simple vested in the United States, so that the Government could at any time close a street or occupy a public square for such purposes as it deemed proper.

The question as to the scope of the deed in this regard came up early in a dispute between the commissioners and the proprietors. The latter thought that the United States had the right only to use the streets as public highways, and not to alienate them, or divert them to other uses.

Attorney-Generals Lee, Breckinridge, Wirt, and Cushing advised that the United States had the fee-simple title to the streets, and avenues, and reservations, and it was so held in the case of Van Ness *et ux. vs.* The City of Washington. (4 Peters, 232.)

Of this grant the Supreme Court says:

The grants were made for the foundation of a Federal city, and the public faith was necessarily pledged when the grants were accepted to found such a city.

Again:

Congress must forever have an interest to protect and aid the city.

The city was designed to last in perpetuity—*Capitoli immobile saxum.*

No imperial government ever possessed greater powers over the soil than was conveyed in this deed.

This absolute control is further seen in the following clause of the deed, which I will notice:

But the said conveyance to the said grantor—

The Government was to reconvey to the grantor what it did not require—

his heirs or assigns, as well as the conveyance and purchase, *shall be on and subject to such terms and conditions as shall be thought reasonable by the President for the time being, for regulating the materials and manner of the buildings, and improvements on the lots generally in the said city, or any particular streets, or parts thereof, for common convenience, safety, and order.*

Here we have the very construction of the houses and the improvements generally subject to the exclusive will of the President.

Can there be any doubt that the purpose of the Government in making this deed was to leave the purchasers of private lots and the proprietors no judgment on, or participation in, the direction of the plan of the city, or its control after being planned?

There was a handful of people here at the time, a few families composing the proprietors of the soil, that were desirous of retaining their present buildings and grounds, and the little graveyard which they had set apart for the home of their dead, but these were not so sacred as to stand in the way of establishing just such a city and upon just such a plan as the President and his commissioners, acting under authority of Congress, should devise; and it was therefore provided, that "in case the arrangement of the streets, lots, and the like will conveniently admit of it," the grantors shall retain their buildings and graveyard by paying at the rate of "twelve pounds ten shillings per acre for the land so retained."

The private owners of lots did not complain then, nor do they now, that the Government possessed itself thus absolutely of every interest of the city; for if the original idea had been consistently carried out, Washington would be to-day the finest metropolis in the world. But what the citizens from the first have had reason to complain of, and what they now complain of, is, that while the Government has in many ways acknowledged its obligations to build here a great Federal city at Federal expense, it has practically thrown almost the whole burden upon private property, as I shall hereafter show.

PLAN OF THE CITY.

The first record evidence of arrangements made for laying out the city of Washington that I have found, is a letter of General Washington, dated March 11, 1791. In a subsequent letter, of April 30, the same year, he speaks of it as the "Federal city," but in a letter of the commissioners, dated September 9, 1791, they informed the architect, Major L'Enfant, that they had agreed to call the Federal district the "Territory of Columbia," and the Federal city the "city of Washington."

L'Enfant was a French officer who sought service here during the Revolution. Having attracted the attention of General Washington he served near his person; but it was probably through the influence of Mr. Jefferson that he was selected as the architect to plan the future Federal city. Mr. Jefferson, who took great interest in the plan, mentions in a letter to Washington that he had furnished L'Enfant with large and accurate maps of all the principal cities of the continent.

To this French officer are we indebted for the general idea ultimately adopted in the plan, although the one adopted finally and reported to Congress, engraved, and circulated through Europe, was prepared by Major Ellicott.

This plan, as agreed upon, was submitted to Congress in the following message, December 13, 1791:

I place before you a plan of the city that has been laid out within the district of ten miles square, which was fixed upon as the permanent seat of the Government.

G. WASHINGTON.

UNITED STATES, *December* 13, 1791.

If members will take the trouble to examine this plan, now on file in the office of Public Buildings and Grounds, all doubt will disappear as to the fact that the Government intended this city to be developed and improved at Government expense.

The evidences of the intention of the Government to make this a great city at Government expense are everywhere apparent. Standing at the site of the Capitol building as the center, we have this immense area divided by wide streets crossing each other at right angles, while radiating to every point of the compass, and in remote parts of the city crossing diagonally the rectangular streets, are broad, magnificent avenues, with many reserved sites for public buildings, and seventeen large reservations for parks, or for Government use, dotting the plan in all parts of the city.

Of these, varying in width from ninety to one hundred and sixty feet, there are one hundred and ninety-five miles of streets and sixty-five miles of avenues; the area thus appropriated to thoroughfares being more than all the area of the reservations and building lots together.

No one looking at the plan would conclude that convenience and economy for transacting business, which are the first considerations in laying out commercial cities, for a moment entered into the minds of the founders of this great city.

That gentlemen may see by comparison of street areas in other cities how far Washington excels them all in its "magnificent distances," I give in this connection the following table:

Ratio of areas of certain cities.

	Per cent.
Paris	25.08
Vienna	35.08
Philadelphia	29.08
Berlin	26.04
Boston	26.02
New York	35.03
Washington	54.05

From this table it will be seen that Paris, thought by many to be the most beautiful city of Europe, notwithstanding its grand boulevards, and its Champs Elysées, has less than one-half the street area of Washington City. The greater part of the business streets of Paris are, for the convenience of business, made narrow, while their avenues and boulevards are broad and beautiful; but here there is not a street less than double the width of Broadway, New York.

That Government ever could have designed to tax private property in this city for the entire improvement of these streets and avenues is to the last degree absurd.

Mr. Wirt, Attorney-General, in speaking of this plan of the city, said:

> I consider sales made under the public exhibition of this plan as amounting to a contract between the public and the individual purchasers, from which it would be unwarrantable to depart.

If the honor of the nation was pledged in this plan, when Congress authorized it to be engraved and sent to the leading cities of Europe, how much more was the honor of the nation pledged that the proceeds of lots should be used to improve the city, as well as that the burden and responsibility of this improvement should fall upon Government.

Every purchaser of Government lots—and Government owned half of all—and every original owner had the right to assume that Government was pledged not only to the plan, but, back of this, to carry out its promises that this should be a Federal city, under Federal protection, and sustained and improved at Federal expense.

The grandeur of this plan, and the magnificent intention of its makers, may further be seen by noticing some of the features embraced in it.

I shall here give the explanations, observations, and references to be found upon the original plan prepared by Major L'Enfant, which is now hanging in the office of General Babcock; the only one in existence, much marred, and scarcely distinguishable in many of its features. I do this as furnishing one of the highest evidences of the purposes of the original founders, and as giving information which is probably unknown to a large number of members.

Observations explanatory of the plan.

First. The positions for the different grand edifices, and for the several grand squares, or areas of different shapes, as they are laid down, were first determined on the most advantageous ground, commanding the most extensive prospect, and the better susceptible of such improvements as the various intents of the several objects may require.

Secondly. Lines or avenues of direct communication have been devised to connect the separate and most distant objects with the principal, and to preserve through the whole a reciprocity of sight at the same time. Attention has been paid to the passing of those leading avenues over the most favorable ground for prospect and convenience.

Thirdly. North and south lines, intersected by others running due east and west, make the distribution of the city into streets, squares, &c., and those lines have been so combined as to meet at certain given points with those divergent avenues, so as to form on the spaces first determined the different squares or areas, which are all proportioned in magnitude to the number of avenues leading to them.

Breadth of streets.

Every grand transverse avenue, and every principal divergent one, such as the communication from the President's House to the Congress House, &c., are one hundred and sixty feet in breadth, and thus divided:

	Feet.
Ten feet of pavement on each side	20
Thirty feet of gravel walk, planted with trees on each side	60
Eighty feet in the middle for carriage-way	80
	160

The other streets are of the following dimensions, to wit:

	Feet.
Those leading to public buildings or markets	130
Others	110
Others	90

L'Enfant then informs us how these lines were drawn. I quote again:

In order to execute the above plan, Mr. Elliott drew a true meridional line by celestial observation, which passes through the area intended for the Congress House. This line is crossed by another line due east and west, which passes through the same area. These lines were accurately measured and made the basis on which the whole plan was executed. He ran all the lines by a transit instrument, and determined the acute angles by actual measurement, and left nothing to the uncertainty of the compass.

I quote again, as showing the grandeur of the idea:

References.

A. The equestrian figure of George Washington; a monument voted in 1783 by the late Continental Congress.

This is the site now occupied by the unfinished Washington Monument.

B. A historic column, also intended for a mile or itinerary column, from whose station (a mile from the Federal House) all distances of places through the continent are to be calculated.

This spot is now what is known as Lincoln Square, near the terminus of East Capitol street.

C. A naval itinerary column, proposed to be erected to celebrate the first rise of the Navy, and to stand a ready monument to consecrate its progress and achievements.

This spot is near the steamboat landing, at the foot of Seventh street.

D. This church is intended for national purposes, such as public prayer, thanksgivings, funeral orations, &c., and assigned to the special use of no particular sect, or denomination, but equally open to all. It will be likewise a proper shelter for such monuments as were voted by the late Continental Congress for those heroes who fell in the cause of liberty, and for such others as may hereafter be decreed by the voice of a grateful nation.

This was to have been our "Westminster Abbey," and its site is now occupied by the Patent Office, while the heroes and sages whose memory was to have been perpetuated in this monumental church lie in unknown graves, unwilling to be mentioned in connection with their country's history, so long as the monument of their leader remains an unfinished, forgotten, and broken column.

E. Five grand fountains intended with a constant spout of water.

N. B. There are within the limits of the city above twenty-five good springs of excellent water, abundantly supplied in the driest season of the year.

These fountains were to have been located: one on Pennsylvania avenue between Twentieth and Twenty-second streets west; another on New York avenue between Twelfth and Thirteenth streets; another on Pennsylvania avenue and Ninth street; one on New Jersey avenue and G street southwest; another on Maryland avenue and Eighth street northeast.

F. Grand cascade formed by the water from the source of the Tiber.

This was at the base of the Capitol.

G. Public walk, being a square of twelve hundred feet, through which carriages may ascend to the upper square of the Federal House.

This is what is now known as the Mall.

H. Grand avenue, four hundred feet in breadth and about a mile in length, bordered with gardens, ending in a slope from the houses on each side. This avenue leads to the Monument, A, and connects the Congress garden with

I. The President's Park, and the

K. Well-improved field, being a part of the walk from the President's House, of about eighteen hundred feet in breadth and of three-fourths of a mile in length. Every lot deep-colored red, with green plats, designates some of the situations which command the most agreeable prospects, and which are the best calculated for spacious houses and gardens, such as may accommodate foreign ministers, &c.

All this ground is familiar to gentlemen of the House. Most of it is occupied for business purposes instead of the spacious dwellings which L'Enfant invited.

L. Around the square, (Capitol Square,) and all along.

M. The avenue from the two bridges to the Federal House, the pavement on each side will pass under an arched way, under whose cover shops will be most conveniently and agreeably situated. This street is one hundred and sixty feet in breadth, and a mile long.

He refers here to Pennsylvania avenue east and East Capitol street, and here we have the only suggestion that the idea of business being transacted in Washington ever entered into the mind of the architect, and he places the shops, as they are found in some European towns, under arcades.

I must remind gentlemen that these are not wild, visionary notions of the French architect which were finally discarded and reduced to plain, practical business notions, such as would govern in laying off a commercial town; but they are ideas which were ultimately crystallized in the shape of legislation, and formed a part of the plighted faith of the nation with regard to its metropolis.

But in this very interesting piece of history, connected with this subject, I must abstract from this original, and to most persons inaccessible, plan some further observations which are recorded upon it, and which form a part of this important history. The architect further says:

The squares colored yellow, being fifteen in number, are proposed to be divided among the several States in the Union for each of them to improve, or subscribe a sum additional to the value of the land for that purpose, and the improvements around the squares to be completed in a limited time.

The center of each square will admit of statues, columns, obelisks, or any other ornaments such as the different States may choose to erect, to perpetuate not only the memory of such individuals whose counsels or military achievements were conspicuous in giving liberty and independence to this country, but also those whose usefulness hath rendered them worthy of general imitation to invite the youth of succeeding generations to tread in the paths of those sages or heroes whom their country has thought proper to celebrate.

The situation of these squares is such that they are the most advantageously and reciprocally seen from each other, and as equally distributed over the whole city district, and connected by spacious avenues around the grand Federal improvements, and as contiguous to them, and at the same time as equally distant from each other as circumstances would admit. The settlements around these squares must soon become connected.

The figures colored red are intended for the use of all religious denominations, on which they are to erect places of worship, and are proposed to be allowed them in the manner as those colored yellow to the different States in the Union, but no burying grounds will be admitted within the limits of the city, an appropriation being intended for that purpose without.

N. B.—There is a number of squares, or areas, unappropriated, and in situations proper for colleges, academies, and of which every society whose object is national may be accommodated.

What a humiliating spectacle, Mr. Chairman, it must have been to those heroes and sages who had passed away from this scene, leaving these grand intentions to be carried out by posterity, to look down upon this Government and behold it selling at public auction for gain the very squares and plats of ground that had been thus sacredly dedicated!

But I shall make but one further extract from this interesting and rare old plan, which is as follows:

This mode of taking possession of and improving the whole district at first must leave to posterity a grand idea of the patriotic interest which promoted it.

What higher evidence could be placed before the committee in support of the proposition which I am now endeavoring to establish?

Patriotic pride could not resist the temptation to remind us that the work which our fathers entered upon was to be handed down as an evidence of the great interest in the future of their country which filled their hearts. Here is the highest declaration of the purpose to take possession of and improve at once as a unit this grand Federal capital, and to leave to posterity in this plan and in this work "a grand idea of the patriotic interest which promoted it."

But I must not longer dwell upon this old plan, the very atmosphere and surroundings of which are redolent with the touch of Washington, and every line and tracing upon which is sacred.

The emotions that must have filled the hearts of the fathers as they saw laid out here a city which in the vision of the future was to illustrate at once the power, grandeur, and glory of the nation, may well be recalled by us at this moment.

When, in November, 1800, Congress assembled here for the first time, President Adams said:

I congratulate the people of the United States on the assembling of Congress at the permanent seat of their government, and I congratulate you, gentlemen, upon the prospect of a residence not to be changed. * * * *

May this Territory be the residence of virtue and happiness; in this city may that piety, fraught with wisdom and magnanimity, that constancy and self-government which adorned the great character whose name it bears, be forever held in veneration. Here and throughout our country may simple manners, pure morals, and true religion flourish forever.

It is for you, gentlemen, to consider whether the local powers of the District of Columbia, vested by the Constitution in the Congress of the United States, shall be immediately exercised. If, in your opinion, this important trust ought now to be executed, *you cannot fail, while performing it, to take into view the probable situation of the Territory, for the happiness of which you are about to provide. You will consider it as the capital of a great nation*, advancing with inexhaustible rapidity in arts, commerce, in wealth, and in population, and possessing within itself those energies and resources which, if not thrown away or lamentably misdirected, will secure to it a long course of prosperity and self-government.

That Mr. Adams, and all who were working with him to place the Government on lasting foundations, regarded this capital city as the "only child of the Union," whose ultimate greatness and grandeur were to depend solely upon the Government, there can be no doubt.

Later, in laying the corner-stone of the Capitol extension, the spirit of the great and good men of the past seized upon Daniel Webster, who upon that interesting occasion said:

> Fellow-citizens, what contemplations are awakened in our minds as we assemble here to re-enact a scene like that performed by Washington. Methinks I see his venerable form now before me, as presented in the glorious statue by Houdon, now in the capitol of Virginia. He is dignified and grave, but concern and anxiety seem to soften the lineaments of his countenance.
>
> The Government over which he presides is yet in the crisis of experiment. Not free from troubles at home, he sees the world in commotion and in arms all around him. He sees that imposing foreign powers are half disposed to try the strength of the recently established American Government. We perceive that mighty thoughts, mingled with fears as well as hopes, are struggling with him. He heads a short procession over these then naked fields, he crosses yonder stream on a fallen tree, he ascends to the top of this eminence, whose original oaks of the forest stand as thick around him as if the spot had been dedicated to Druidical worship. And here he performs the appointed duty of the day.

But let me advance in the argument.

CONTEMPORANEOUS ACTS AND VIEWS.

I am endeavoring, Mr. Chairman, to show to the committee that but one purpose animated the founders of the capital, which was to make it a magnificent metropolis at the Federal expense. In the overwhelming array of facts and circumstances clearly establishing this proposition, I shall next present some contemporaneous acts and expressions of those most prominent in carrying out the wishes of Congress.

In March, 1791, Washington, in a letter to Mr. Jefferson, written from Mount Vernon, felicitated himself upon having reconciled the contending interests of land-owners, and of "uniting them in such an agreement *as permits* the *public purposes* to be carried into effect on an *extensive* and *proper scale*."

In his reply, Mr. Jefferson declares the acquisitions to be "really noble," and adds, "I think very liberal reserves should be made for the public."

Again, writing to the commissioners of the city of Washington, he says:

> When you are in the situation to begin opening the avenues, it is presumed those which will be more immediately useful will be first cleared.

While executing the wishes of Congress with regard to the capital, the President found it necessary to make a loan from the State of Maryland. His correspondence shows how deeply interested he was, and what anxious solicitude he felt for the growth and prosperity of the city; and his entire intercourse with the commissioners exhibits a fraternal feeling toward this child of the Union utterly inconsistent with any idea that it was to be built by private citizens. Washington did not, however, live to witness the fulfillment of his wishes. He died on the 14th of December, 1799, nearly a year before the Government occupied the capital he had contributed so much to found.

I have already called attention to President Adams's opening speech to Congress on its assembling in Washington, in which he spoke of this city as the capital of a great nation, for the happiness of which Congress was to provide.

The Senate replied:

> We meet you, sir, and the other branch of the national Legislature, in the city which is honored by the name of our late hero and sage, the illustrious Washington

with sensations and emotions which exceed our power of description. * * * * Great indeed would have been our gratification if his sum of earthly happiness had been completed by seeing the Government thus peaceably convened at this place. * * * * The question whether the legal powers over the District of Columbia, vested by the Constitution in the Congress of the United States, shall be immediately exercised, is of great importance, and in deliberating upon it we shall naturally be led to weigh the attending circumstances and every probable consequence of the measures which may be proposed.

The House replied:

A consideration of those powers which have been vested in Congress over the District of Columbia will not escape our attention, nor shall we forget that in exercising these powers a regard must be had to those events which will necessarily attend the capital of America.

But without extending these contemporaneous expressions, allow me to read an extract from an article in the Philadelphia Herald of the 4th of January, 1795. This article is a general review of the plan of the city, and commences as follows:

To found a city in the center of the United States, for the purpose of making it a depository of the acts of the Union and the sanctuary of the laws which must one day rule all North America, is a grand and comprehensive idea, which has already become with propriety the object of public respect. In reflecting on the importance of the Union, and on the advantages which it secures to all the inhabitants of the United States collectively or to individuals, where is there an American who does not see, in the establishment of a Federal town, a natural means for confirming forever that valuable connection to which the nation is indebted for liberation from the British yoke? The Federal city, situated in the center of the United States, is a temple erected to liberty, and toward this edifice will the wishes and expectations of all true friends, of every country, be necessarily directed. *The city of Washington, considered under such important points of view, could not be calculated on a small scale. Its extent, the disposition of its avenues and public squares, should all correspond with the magnitude of the object for which it was intended; and we need only cast our eyes upon the situation and plan of the city to recognize in them the comprehensive genius of the President, to whom the direction of the business has been committed by Congress.*

Here, I think, Mr. Chairman, is the absolute proof of my proposition, that contemporaneously with the location of the seat of government it was the well-understood purpose of its founders to establish a city which was to be national, and in whose growth and prosperity the whole country was to take an interest.

This city was to be a grand civic monument—the one spot in which were to be gathered the treasures of succeeding ages, and whatever might tend to strengthen the Union, and combine in one patriotic bond the whole people of the nation.

LEGISLATION OF CONGRESS.

Prior to June 1, 1802, the government of the city was in a board of commissioners, created by the act of the 16th of July, 1790, but on May 1, 1802, an act passed abolishing the office of commissioners and providing that the affairs of the city should be thereafter under the direction of a superintendent, to be appointed by the President.

The improvements of the city were made directly by the United States, and to aid in this a city fund was started from the proceeds of the sale of lots by the United States, which it was thought at the time would, by judicious management, go far toward the development of the magnificent intentions of the founders. And the act to which I have just alluded directed a sale of lots to re-enforce this city fund.

President Jefferson, January 11, 1802, in a message to Congress, says:

If indulgence for the funds can be admitted, these lots will probably form a reserve of great and permanent value.

He further says:

That if the sale is forced for the payment of Government loans he fears the whole property will be sacrificed, and the residuary interest of the city entirely lost.

I understand this residuary interest to be none other than a right to the proceeds of the sale of lots for the purpose of improving the city.

The act of March 3, 1803, fixes the salary of the superintendent and of the surveyor of the city, and makes appropriation for the expenses of their offices, to be paid out of the city funds; but these funds, as we have seen, arose from the proceeds of lots belonging to the United States. This same act appropriates from the Treasury of the United States $50,000, among other things, "for keeping in repair the highway between the Capitol and other public buildings."

Up to this time the government of the city, in all its details, was directly by legislation of Congress. It was found, however, that the growing wants of this young city would require certain local municipal legislation, which it would be inconvenient always to be obliged to apply to Congress for, and the inhabitants were given a charter of incorporation. The mayor was appointed by the President, and the council elected by the free white male tax-payers. The usual powers were conferred, except, however, that no authority was extended over the streets and avenues, other than that the corporation was permitted "to keep them in repair, agreeably to the plan of the said city." This charter expired two years after its creation, and was renewed from time to time until March 5, 1820, when a charter of more extended powers was granted. Meanwhile the interests of the United States passed into the control of an officer known as the Commissioner of Public Buildings and Grounds—now the engineer in charge of public buildings and grounds.

Gradually, as the city increased in population and the Government became absorbed in the consideration of great national questions, and largely owing also to attempts to revive the question of removal of the capital, Congress seemed to have drifted away from its early policy, and left the question of local improvements entirely to the citizens. I do not find that between 1807 and 1823 the Government had expended a single dollar upon the improvements of the streets. The fund arising from the sale of lots, instead of being used for the improvement of the city, was almost entirely devoted to the erection of public buildings.

The revenues of Government in that day were small, and Congress probably found itself compelled to divert the improvement fund, throwing the burden upon private property, or leaving the realization of the early intentions as to the capital to be worked out by posterity.

That by these acts of incorporation permission was given the citizens to carry out the great work which the Government was itself obliged by every consideration of honor to do, is no answer to the argument. If the Government, when poor, could not do this work or encourage the citizens to do it, now, that the Government has grown powerful and rich and amply able to remove the burden to its own shoulders, I insist that the obligation is even stronger to do so. But I was noticing the legislation as tending to establish my proposition; and although the Government has stood by and seen the private property of this District taxed almost to confiscation in the effort to make the city what its founders designed it should be, and has scarcely lent a helping hand, still its legislation nowhere denies its obligations, but on the contrary, whenever any has been passed, it has been in recognition of the theory I am endeavoring to establish.

In the charter of 1820 the Commissioner of Public Buildings is directed—

To reimburse to the said corporation a just proportion of any expense which may hereafter be incurred in laying open, paving, or otherwise improving any of the streets or avenues in front of, &c., any of the public squares or reservations, * * * out of any moneys arising from the sale of lots in the city of Washington belonging to the United States.

A similar provision was in the act of May, 1826, and the act of 1848, and there was in this last act a still stronger recognition of the duty of the Government. The twelfth section provides that the Commissioner of Public Buildings shall—

From time to time cause to be opened and improved such avenues and streets, or parts or portions thereof, as the President of the United States shall deem necessary for the public convenience, and he shall defray the expenses thereof out of any money arising, or which shall have arisen, from the sale of lots in the city of Washington belonging, or which may have belonged, to the United States.

The act also directs the Commissioner to keep in repair certain pavements, gutters, footways, &c., around the public squares, reservations, and other property of the Government. Here we have a full recognition of the obligations of Government, but unfortunately the fund mentioned had disappeared, mainly on the public buildings, and by the improvident disposition of the lots had diminished by millions of dollars, so that practically this liberal provision of Congress did little toward its object.

In this review let me return a moment to the action of the Twenty-third Congress.

The city had made such efforts to improve its condition and do the work which the Government had assumed in the beginning that it had incurred an indebtedness of nearly $2,000,000. Its resources had become so exhausted and its burden so great that it was compelled to appeal to Congress for aid. Its Holland creditors were threatening to foreclose on the property, and, as was said in the debates in the Senate on the subject by one of the Senators, "the capital of the nation was about to be sold out to the Dutch." Up to this time the total expenditures of the Government for the improvement of the streets was $208,925.67½, all of which, with the exception of about $10,000, was for the improvement of Pennsylvania avenue and the streets immediately around and adjoining the Capitol and President's Square. Throughout the whole city the Government had expended, with this exception, for its improvement, up to December, 1834, only about $10,000, while it had received from the sale of lots about $750,000. The neglect of Government to carry out its plighted faith, and the extraordinary efforts of the city to discharge the obligations of Government, attracted the attention of Congress at that time, and the subject was thoroughly examined and reported upon to the Senate February 2, 1835.

The report of the committee, Mr. Southard, chairman, goes quite fully into the relations existing between the capital and the Government.

As Congress sanctioned the report of the committee in the highest possible form, by coming to the relief of the city, the positions assumed by Mr. Southard may be regarded as giving the legislative expression of the Congress of that day, and we may well consider what some of these views were. Mr. Southard says that in improving the streets the city authorities "have been misled into expenditures which did not properly belong to them, although," he adds, "the views by which they were governed were of a liberal and public-spirited character." He refers to the unusual magnitude and extent of the city; the great width of the avenues and streets; the creation of the city in that short space of time, and the pressure for public improvements being sudden; that the population is but twenty thousand, more than half of which are people of color and temporary residents, contributing nothing to the city revenue; that, in addition to the large expenditures made from the city treasury for improvement of streets, the citizens have been compelled to create their market-houses, infirmaries, water privileges, lamps, fire-engines and houses, and pay their police, and the like expenses, and adds:

The committee are of the opinion that the Government was bound by every principle of equal right and justice to pay a proportion of the expenses incurred upon this subject equal to the amount of property which it held, and which was to be increased in value and benefited by it, and this would have been greatly more than one-half. If the streets are its property and to be regarded as altogether under its control, it is not easy to perceive why it should call upon or permit others to keep that property in order; and if the streets are to be regarded as for the joint convenience of the Government and the inhabitants, the expenses of maintaining them should be joint, and in proportion to their respective interests; and that the early action of the Government was in conformity to this principle.

The committee notice also that the immense property of Government, which has been equally benefited by improvement, has been at all times free from taxation, while the property of individuals adjoining it has been subject thereto; that in several States of the Union, where the Government holds landed estate, it has paid taxes upon it, and those taxes have been expended for the ordinary municipal purposes of the place where the same is situated. The hardship to private property-holders in exemption of Government property from taxation is strikingly illustrated when we remember that the Government has been the owner of lots held for sale ever since the capital was located here, and yet these lots not reserved for public use, but held by the Government for speculation, have paid no taxes. The committee conclude their report as follows:

In the investigation of the subject committed to them, and of the relief to be proposed, the committee have been unable to separate the interests of the District from the interests of the United States. They regard it as the child of the Union, as the creation of the Union for its own purposes. That the design of the Constitution and its founders was to create a residence for the Government, where they should have absolute and unlimited control, which should be regulated and governed by them without the interference of partial interests in the States; which should be built up and sustained by their authority and resources, not dependent upon the will or resources of any State or local interest.

If this had not been the design, a temporary or permanent seat of government would have been selected in some populous city, or some territory, subject to State jurisdiction; and, if this was the design, it is not easy to comprehend either the principle which would prevent the Government from a liberal appropriation of the national resources to accomplish the object, or the policy which could confine the city to the means possessed by the inhabitants for its improvement.

This report is important in many particulars, but more than all in this one, to wit, that it forms the connecting link between the present period and the revolutionary period, and embodies at once the record evidence as well as the tradition and common understanding and belief of the founders of the Republic and those who immediately succeeded them. I believe that upon this evidence any court would convict the United States of a palpable and gross violation of its original purpose in founding this capital city; and the subsequent congressional history as touching this subject confirms the fact, that while in theory this principle has always been acknowledged, in practice it has been almost entirely ignored. But an examination of this legislative history will show that at different periods absorbing subjects have drawn the public mind away from the capital as a national object, but it has been one of the results of the recent war that public attention has returned again to this city. An examination of the statutes will show that more than four times as much money has been appropriated by the Forty-first and Forty-second Congresses for improvements in the city as during the previous seventy years. But I cannot longer dwell upon this branch of my subject.

I think if any question is susceptible of demonstration not mathematical, yet absolutely certain, the one which I started out to prove may now be placed in that category. I have shown the history of the location of the capital, the purpose of its founders, and the obligations of the United States in relation to it. I have now to notice what has actually been done by Government, what has been done by the municipal authorities, and what it is the duty of the national Government still to do.

SOME ERRORS CORRECTED.

A common error prevails over the whole country that the United States at this time pays all the expense of the government of the District of Columbia and the improvements at the capital. Within a week I have been asked by persons high in official position if the United States did not pay for our recent improvements.

Now, Mr. Chairman, I propose to lay bare the short-comings of Government, and place its neglect side by side with the efforts made by private citizens. We are set down as a miserable community of paupers and beggars, hanging on the skirts of Congress for sustenance; whereas the truth is the United States for the past seventy years have kept this people down in a condition of vassalage, squeezing the last possible penny out of them to carry on the very work which the founders of the capital had pledged their faith should be done by the United States.

The United States have stood by and have seen their capital become a by-word and scoffing throughout the civilized world. They have seen the shafts of scorn and contempt and satire pointed toward it without making a single creditable effort to avert them.

Not only this, but they have themselves largely contributed to the condition of things which, until within a few years, made us a just object of contempt.

We shall find in this examination of what has been done and left undone a striking evidence of the utter want of unity of purpose and design on the part of the Government in its exercise of control over this District.

For thirty years it did little more than hew out some paths to the public buildings, and stake off the streets and avenues for the people of the District to improve; the exact amount expended by Government in this period being $20,000—less than $700 a year.

Who can defend this miserable parsimony, and who can justify the conduct of Government in this trifling with a great public duty imposed upon it by the founders of the capital, especially when it is remembered that during the same period it had realized $700,000 from the improvident sale of lots—funds which had been pledged for the benefit of improvements?

Look at your superb Capitol building. There has never been a moment since it was erected when its surroundings would compare favorably with a New England barn-yard. Twelve million dollars in this marble pile, of grand promise without and disappointment within, but surrounded worse than a western court-house. It only lacks a horse-block and hitching-rack to make it perfectly primitive and rural.

Look at the original plan of the city, which drew forth eulogiums from all quarters of the globe, and which occupied many of the best hours of many early patriots, and see how it has been hacked and defaced.

With no common feeling of pride in the capital pervading the country, and thus through the people reaching Congress, and with no one to protest against encroachments upon the idea which found expression in the original plan, the surprise is rather that we have a city left at all of sufficient proportions and form to elicit the admiration of any one.

It has been charged also that we are here not only supported by Government, but that we are an unproductive, thriftless community, drawing from and giving back nothing to Government. When we ask aid, the question is treated from a local stand-point and not a national one, and appropriations are always heralded as so much money given to the people of the District; whereas every dollar expended here by Government is more closely brought home to every citizen of the country than an appropriation in any form that can be named. This is the only spot common to the whole people on the face of our vast empire, where the humblest citizen can come and claim he is in the midst of his own, and where he feels he has a personal pecuniary interest in everything he beholds.

But, sir, I will not allow the impression to go uncontradicted that we feed upon and do not nourish Government. The truth will show that these District barnacles and leeches are the most remarkable of their genus.

The report of the Commissioner of the Internal-Revenue Bureau for 1873 shows (page 153) that the District of Columbia, since 1863, has paid, exclusive of tax on income, into the United States Treasury, $4,695,119.94—more than all the other Territories combined; more than Arkansas, Florida, Kansas, Minnesota, Nebraska, Nevada, or Oregon; *and more than the expenditures of the United States for improvement of the capital since its foundation.* In ten years this tax-burdened District has more than reimbursed the Government for every dollar laid out here for the common benefit of its own and private property.

Need I stop to apply these facts to remove the false impression I am combating?

It would seem to the natural vision that these leeches and barnacles would be profitable to Government if the species could be propagated and sent into some of the States.

Mr. Chairman, this city belongs to the United States. It cannot be wiped out without giving a vital blow to the Government. It cannot be trampled under foot without visiting a wrong upon every man, woman, and child in the nation. It cannot be longer ignored without humiliation and shame. A combination of events has brought the duty of Congress prominently before the country, and members must reach some conclusion, and it must be one they can defend before the world.

I have read the press closely since we have been placed in the crucible, and I say that even the papers most unfair and prejudiced against the *personnel* of our local government and its management, take a high patriotic stand when speaking of the duty of Congress. I have yet to find a paper which advocates the narrow view that the United States shall do nothing toward improving and beautifying the nation's capital, especially as the Government owns half the real estate and possesses absolute proprietary control over every street, avenue, alley, square, park, and reservation in it. Even Mr. Dana's Sun, whose columns pour red-hot lava upon the heads of our officers daily, has never suggested that Congress should stand by and see our people taxed out of their homes to improve Government property, but, on the contrary, has urged just what I urge, that it is the duty of Congress to contribute its just proportion of the municipal expenses.

I appeal to every member of this House whose constituents have visited this city within the last year whether they have not gone home believing it to be the duty of Government to aid in making Washington the pride of the nation; and I appeal to him also to tell me whether he has not blushed with shame when obliged to tell them howl ittle the United States have done to place the capital where it now is.

Why, sir, France expended $15,000,000 to open the Boulevard Sebastopol, in Paris, and yet we must plead as for a charity when we ask this rich people to make a just, fixed, and certain appropriation annually to carry on improvements in which the whole country are interested.

I confess, Mr. Chairman, I weary of this contest year after year to obtain simple justice for the District of Columbia. I weary of the indifference of Congress to the plighted faith of the nation. I weary of the abject dependence of this community and the position of obsequiousness which their agent must submit to lest he offend some congressional propriety or step on some congressional toe. I weary of combating the assumption that the District of Columbia has no rights which Congressmen are bound to respect; and I would turn hopelessly away from these Halls if I did not see around me republicans and democrats who will never willingly see Congress fasten upon this people a perpetual bondage as the result of their unexampled efforts to redeem the nation's capital from disgrace.

No, Mr. Chairman, it is a broader question we are discussing than mere aid to a community; it is whether the plans and purposes of the early fathers shall be carried out and the country's faith be kept; it is whether you shall have here the finest public buildings in the world, and shall hold half of the soil in reservations, and all the streets and avenues in fee, and yet do nothing to light your city, to pave its streets, to protect your houses and Departments from fire and from robbers, to secure proper sanitary protection—in short, whether you will adopt a wise, patriotic, consistent, and well-defined policy toward the capital, and will act with some reference to the common pride in it which all intelligent Americans feel.

STATEMENT OF THE ACCOUNT.

Now, Mr. Chairman, let me endeavor to present to the House the exact expenditures of the general and local government in the District of Columbia for improvements, such as we think should be shared by both governments in some just proportion.

I have obtained from the Treasury Department a statement of the expenditures of the General Government since 1800, and it is of such value in this discussion that I shall spread it at length before the House and the country. It gives the amount, as shown by vouchers in the Treasury Department, expended by Government upon streets and avenues in the way of improvements. I shall omit the description of the purpose for which the appropriation is made, remarking generally that the items cover pavements, sewers, sidewalks, bridges in the city on canal, and Tiber Creek, grading, &c.

Statement of expenditures on account of improvements of avenues and streets in the city of Washington, from 1800 to 1871, inclusive.

Year	Amount
1800	$10,000 00
1823	5,000 00
1824	5,000 00
1832	60,000 00
1833	76,680 00
1834	9,233 70
1838	2,280 00
1842	12,000 00
1843	3,933 26
1846	10,000 00
1848	16,000 00
1849	3,754 11
1850	26,286 50
1851	44,845 64
1852	36,277 33
1853	15,329 37
1854	36,933 77
1855	17,666 69
1856	7,229 58
1857	17,500 00
1858	15,000 00
1859	6,550 00
1860	3,000 00
1861	13,518 87
1862	3,300 00
1863	11,846 13
1864	13,223 66
1865	8,926 58
1866	56,841 88
1867	72,973 69
1868	20,100 00
1869	321,575 00
1870	2,051 76
1871	10,000 00
Total	1,002,785 52

In 1832–'33 Congress had an improvement spasm, and expended in laying a cobble-stone pavement on Pennsylvania avenue $136,680; and, having thus secured a communication between the President's House and the Capitol, relapsed into its usual indifference, and for the next thirty years did comparatively nothing.

In 1869 the wooden-pavement period began here, by a compulsory law of Congress, requiring owners of property abutting on Pennsylvania avenue to pave it with that costly material. To this forerunner of the new era for Washington Congress contributed $321,575. The appropriation for 1870, immediately following this, was $2,051.76, and strikingly illustrates the utter lack of a policy toward the District, or any comprehension of its needs.

Then came the new District government and the Forty-second Congress, and with them a regeneration of the capital.

Since George Washington consecrated the seat of government, and John Adams baptized it in the name of the patriot fathers, no Congress has shown anything like the intelligent, practical, and patriotic devotion to the nation's capital exhibited by the Forty-second Congress. It placed to the credit of the improvement fund $3,597,801.18 —more than three times the amount voted by the forty-one preceding Congresses, while the citizens submitted their property and purses cheerfully to the awful demand of the board of public works, and gave in two years $11,175,978.76, which, added to previous expenditures of the District—$9,199,431.94—makes the appalling sum of $20,375,410.70!

Now, compare the two governments, local and national. The former has expended an average since 1800 of more than six times the amount expended by the latter.

There never has been a time when the interest of Government here was not equal to that of the private property-holders, even if we look at the question in its narrowest form. The account, therefore, at this point would stand thus:

Expended by District of Columbia	$20, 375, 410 70
Expended by Government	4, 600, 586 70
	15, 774, 824 00
To reimburse District of Columbia excess of expenditures one-half of difference	7, 887, 412 00

To make the account square, Congress should appropriate this sum.

This is the exact statement of the account between the national and local governments at this time in the matter of improvements of streets and avenues, including the system of sewers.

The expenditures of the national Government I have upon the authority of the Secretary of the Treasury; and the expenditures of the local government upon the authority of the governor of the District, in his return to the present committee of investigation, printed page 461.

To further illustrate the share which Government has borne of the ordinary necessary expenses of the city, let me notice some of the branches of the local service separately. I have heretofore claimed that the United States should bear at least half of the municipal expenses of the District of Columbia. I do this upon the evidence which is to be found throughout the whole period of our history, that the interest of the General Government has always been regarded as at least half of that of the local government. It was so treated by Congress in 1835. (See report of Senator Southard, February 2, 1835.) It was so treated in 1858. (See report of Senator Brown, May 15, 1858.) And the recent careful valuation confirms this apportionment. (See Governor Shepherd's answer, pages 461, 462.)

When the founders laid off this capital city, they must have contemplated that at some time, beside paved streets and sewers, it would need a police force; a supply of water; means for lighting the streets; a board of health officers for sanitary protection; a fire department; a system of common schools; and, in short, the usual requisites for securing health and protection common to great cities. They saw that while these were wants of any city, they would, from the nature of the plan of this one, be greatly augmented, and much more than ordinarily expensive. The broad streets and avenues, and the frequently recurring public squares and parks, necessarily contemplated a city here whose inhabitants would be widely scattered over the area.

To protect such a community by proper police, by fire department, sewers, gas, and the other comforts of city life, it would necessarily be more expensive to the inhabitants than in those densely crowded cities where the same facilities would reach a much larger number at the same cost. And we have here another reason for concluding that the original purpose was to hold the Government responsible, in part at least, for securing these necessary privileges.

I propose briefly, in this connection, to present to the committee, as near as I am able, from data which I have procured from officers of the Government and from Federal records, precisely what the local and what the national Government has done in this regard.

POLICE.

On the 23d of August, 1842, an act of Congress was approved organizing the police force known as the "Auxiliary Guard."

Previous to this that service had been performed by constables, whose compensation was derived from fees. The Auxiliary Guard was paid exclusively by the General Government, and was increased from time to time by acts of Congress, until August, 1861, when the present Metropolitan police was substituted; and for the better protection of the interests of Government the United States assumed entire police control within the District.

For three years, to June 30, 1864, this force was paid exclusively by the United States, when by an act of Congress the number of employés of the board of police was increased 50 per cent., but the act required the local authorities of the District to pay for this increase.

On the 11th of March, 1851, the corporation of Washington organized a salaried police force, consisting of fifteen men, and in 1858 increased the number to twenty-five. This was the first and only police force organized by the local authorities, and continued until the organization of the Metropolitan police. The chief of this department, Major Richards, informs me that by an approximate estimate, which he has been able to make from official records, he finds that the United States have paid for police service in the District, since August 23, 1842, to the expiration of the present fiscal year, about $2,400,000. The cost of the police force to the local authorities since March 11, 1851, has been about $1,148,643.33. Here we have the highest recognition of the duty of Government to aid in the payment of municipal expenses. Here the obligation is fully acknowledged and fully discharged; but while the wisdom and justice of it must be admitted, it will seem strange to members that this is the only department of the local government adequately sustained, and, with one or two exceptions, the only department in the least assisted.

WATER DEPARTMENT.

March 3, 1859, Congress enacted a law for the preservation of the works constructed by the United States for bringing the Potomac water into the cities of Washington and Georgetown, for supplying the water for all Government purposes, and for the use and benefit of the inhabitants of said cities.

The act extended to Washington and Georgetown the right to supply their inhabitants with Potomac water from the aqueduct mains, and to make laws and regulations for its distribution, subject to the restrictions of the act of Congress, and it was specially provided that *no expense should devolve upon the United States in consequence of this distribution;* and the act further provides that *whenever the supply of water is found no more than adequate to meet the wants of the General Government, the engineer in charge of the water-works shall stop the supply to the said cities.* The same act authorized the corporations to fix the water rates, and provided that they should *never be a source of revenue,* other than sufficient to provide a supply of water.

A later act of Congress authorized the corporations to levy a tax to pay for mains which they might lay for the supply of the inhabitants.

But I am informed by the water registrar of the District, Colonel Lubey, that the revenues derived from water rents have barely met the outlay.

Here we find that the supply of water brought to the city at the expense in the first instance of the General Government, was done for their sole use; and although afterward it was ascertained that the supply was ample for the use of the Government and the inhabitants, and the corporations were allowed to avail themselves of it, Congress nevertheless reserved the exclusive control over the right to the water as against the inhabitants.

The United States have expended upon the water-works about $3,500,000, while the inhabitants of the District, in laying mains, the erection of fire-plugs, hydrants, &c., have expended about $1,500,000. The daily consumption of water in both cities is eighteen million gallons, of which it is estimated that the Departments of Government use and waste fully one-half. No more important or useful improvement has been undertaken by Government. The result has been to bring an inexhaustible supply of water to the capital at a cost of three and a half millions. This is certainly gratifying when it is remembered that the city of Baltimore expended for a like purpose over four millions; Boston twelve millions; Brooklyn twelve millions; Philadelphia six millions; and New York City over twenty millions.

GAS.

The Washington Gas-light Company was chartered in 1848, and since the use of gas here the United States has paid for lighting streets and avenues $272,340.40. The corporation of Washington and the board of public works have paid $415,087.29 The gas was introduced into Georgetown in February, 1854. The corporation paid for gas supplied to 175 lamps, from 1857 to 1866, $38,965.30. During that period the United States caused to be erected 115 lamps on Bridge and High streets, and paid for gas to supply the same, $34,650.45, but refused after 1866 to light them longer. The corporation thereafter paid the expense to 1871, amounting to $28,991.50, after which the territorial government increased the number of lamps, and paid up to July 1, 1873, $21,698.40. Total paid in Georgetown by local authorities, $85,340.35. Total paid by the United States in Georgetown, $38,465.30. Formerly, and until a recent period, the United States paid for lighting their squares and the lamps around them, Pennsylvania avenue, and other streets, but these are all now lighted by the District government. With the exception of 103 lamps at the President's House and around the Capitol building, every lamp in the District is paid for by the District government. In 1868 the General Government refused to light Four-and-a-half, Sixth, and Twelfth streets, across the Mall, and in 1870 refused to light the avenues, and in 1872 refused to light the streets bordering upon the public squares, and in 1873 ceased to light inside of the squares. At one time the Government paid for 715 lamps, and now but for 103, while the District is paying for 3,130, at an annual cost of about $150,000.

I need not speak of the uses of gas, or of its indispensability, both to the Government and to the city. All must concede this, when it is remembered that not only the comfort of those here in the service of the Government demands the use of it, but the safety of the Government buildings and Government interests generally make its use indispensable; and yet substantially the whole burden is now thrown upon the citizens.

HEALTH DEPARTMENT.

No one can deny that a sanitary and health department is of equal importance to the general as well as the local government.

The United States are morally responsible for securing to their servants at the capital, not only every proper and needed comfort, but protection against disease so far as it is possible. The United States are also responsible for securing the protection and health and comfort of foreign ministers resident at the capital; and these two interests, mentioning no other, are always large and increasing; but until the last Congress made an appropriation, I have been unable to discover any expenditure on the part of the General Government to support our health department.

I have not been able to ascertain what the local government expended prior to our organic act. Our present very efficient board of health is a department of the General Government.

Congress has appropriated for its uses	$69, 000
The District government has appropriated	83, 000

FIRE DEPARTMENT.

Many years ago Congress made a small appropriation for erecting an engine-house in the western part of the city, and later a similar appropriation for the engine-house of the Columbia fire company near the Capitol.

During the rebellion the United States maintained at the capital what was known as the Government fire brigade, composed of three steam fire-engine companies; but it was independent and separate from the city fire department, and was kept with reference more particularly to the protection of Government property. They remained here five years; but the brigade was disbanded in 1869, and the engines sent away from the city.

The present city fire department was organized in 1865, and has cost the city of Washington, since its organization to the present time, $605,000. At least two more engines are very much needed. With more valuable interests to protect than any city in the country, and with a larger area in proportion to the population, we have a smaller fire department than any city in the Union of our population. In this department the United States has taken no interest whatever, and contributes to it absolutely nothing; and yet the scattered records of the Government in all parts of the city, exposed daily to fire, are of incalculable value.

PUBLIC SCHOOLS.

From an early day efforts have been made to attract the attention of Congress to the importance of sustaining here at the capital a common-school system. When the Government entered upon its land-grant policy in aid of education, efforts were made to obtain a grant for this District; and I believe the Senate passed a bill for that purpose, but it failed in the House.

The atmosphere of Washington in those days was not favorable to common schools; and besides the District then, as now, was looked upon as of little consequence, and by its very abject attitude toward the Government inspired contempt rather than interest or pride.

Public schools dragged along without any assistance from Government, and in 1861 cost the city $26,000.

With the war came a vigorous growth in population, mainly from the North. Finding no free schools here worthy the name, they united their efforts with the local authorities and enlarged the school facilities, and increased the school fund, so that I find that during the three years commencing 1870 the total expenditures for this purpose reached the sum of $1,095,000. With absolutely no school property worth mentioning in 1861, we now own real estate amounting to over $1,000,000.

In 1861 the number of pupils attending public schools could not have exceeded 4,500, and included no persons of color. Since 1863 the city of Washington has extended facilities to this class of children, so that there are four thousand colored pupils on the rolls now. Besides paying the current expenses of their schools, permanent building sites have been purchased, and school-buildings have been erected for them to the value of $250,000.

While I cannot go into this subject fully, but must refer to the argument addressed to the Forty-second Congress, to be found in the Globe of January 27, 1872, I will be pardoned for pointing out a few of the reasons why the General Government should aid our public schools. I think no one will question that we have done all in our power to make the school facilities adequate to the needs of the community; and yet the startling fact remains that there are in the city of Washington of school age 25,935 persons, while there are seats provided for only 11,910, leaving 14,025 persons without the benefit of public schools. Of this number 6,759 are reported by the Commissioner of Education as pupils in private schools, leaving 7,266 absolutely destitute of all school privileges.

Why should the Government assist in educating these children? I answer—

First. That the superintendent of schools reports that upon an examination he finds only 26.82 per cent. of parents or guardians of pupils are tax-payers; or, in other words, 73.18 of the parents whose children attend school pay no taxes. I am aware that generally a considerable percentage of parents whose children attend public schools do not pay taxes, but the percentage here is so unusually large as to challenge attention, and I think that when the reason for it is known a strong argument will be discovered in favor of Government aid.

Secondly. In the report of the superintendent for 1872–'73 a table is given, from which I find that of the children attending public schools in the city 3,037 were the children of parents in Government employment, or 30.79 per cent. Some of these persons pay taxes, but a comparatively small number. Usually they have no income but their salary, and the uncertain tenure of office deters them from investing in real estate.

Thirdly. From the same report I find that 32.46 per cent. of the school population are colored, and an examination of the United States census will show that this large proportion is due to the results of political causes, rather than to any economic or social law. Most of them were invited here by the laws of Congress which first gave them freedom, and next the ballot, and where they have felt peculiarly under the protection of the Government, and they now number about one-third of the whole population. From no fault of their own, but rather by reason of their peculiar condition—due to the laws of the country—they are unable to assist very materially in supporting the common-school system.

These two classes which I have named have a right to demand of the General Government some provision for school advantages.

Education here should be free as air, and the District government will never discriminate against any one class, but it will continue to demand of Congress some assistance in this direction. The embarrassment to the District government which we find running through its whole system is here felt even more than elsewhere, to wit, that so large a portion of the property of the District is exempt from taxation.

The United States have no right to expect, and ought not to expect, to retain the services of honest, faithful public servants at low salaries, and force them to live at a place where they will have none of the comforts or necessities of life, or the privileges which will enable them to rear their families properly. Nor have the United States any right, moral or other, to hold out special inducements to any class of our fellow-citizens, inviting them to take up their residence under the shadow and protection of Government at its capital, and cast the whole burden of taxation to furnish these persons with educational advantages and privileges upon the private citizens.

But aside from these special considerations, the policy of the Government, long established, should control its action in this matter. It has already given in aid of public schools nearly one hundred million acres of public lands. Over thirty-four and one-half million acres have gone to the other Territories. We have a greater school population than some of these Territories ever can have. Besides this magnificent land grant, other special and valuable assistance has been extended to the States and Territories in aid of education.

At one time $37,000,000, the proceeds of public lands, were distributed to the States, and much of it for the benefit of public education. It cannot be that the District of Columbia was excluded because it has contributed nothing to the support of Government; for an examination will show that this District has paid into the Internal-Revenue Bureau since its organization, as I have shown, more than all the other Territories combined, and more than several of the States that might be named. I am utterly at a loss to discover any reason for refusing aid, while there are many that must appear convincing why the Government should aid this important work.

I have been unable to ascertain the cost of public schools prior to 1860, but since that time to the present the total expense has been $2,168,000 The Government has not paid one penny, and its donation of a lot, formerly General Jackson's stable-lot, made some years ago, did not exceed in value $1,000.

ACCOUNT—SECOND STATEMENT.

I have thus, Mr. Chairman, gone over about all the expenses which enter into the local government, and I will again state the account with the United States, as affected by the items just mentioned:

Expended by old corporations and the new government for improvements since 1800	$20, 375, 410 70
Expended by same for police department	1, 148, 643 33
Expended by same for water department	1, 500, 000 00
Expended by same for gas department	415, 087 29
Expended by same for health department	83, 000 00
Expended by same for fire department	605, 000 00
Expended by same for public schools, (since 1860)	2, 168, 000 00
Total expended by local government	26, 295, 141 32
Expended by General Government for improvements since 1800	$4, 600, 586 70
Expended by same for police department	2, 400, 000 00
Expended by same for water department	3, 500, 000 00
Expended by same for gas department	272, 340 00
Expended by same for health department	69, 000 00
Expended by same for fire department	....
Expended by same for public schools	....
Total expended by General Government	10, 841, 926 70

ACCOUNT—THIRD STATEMENT.

I know, Mr. Chairman, it is claimed that our citizens enjoy the public parks and reservations in common with Government, and that we should make some allowance for the amount expended heretofore exclusively by Government upon these public grounds. I suppose, however, that no one would insist that the citizens should share the expense of the grounds immediately connected with the Departments, the Capitol, and President's House. But, to leave no room for cavil, I have procured from General Babcock a statement of appropriations made by acts of Congress for the improvements in the parks, reservations, and grounds around the public buildings since December, 1834. Prior to that time I have ascertained the expenditures for this purpose from the report of the Commissioner of Public Buildings and Grounds, appended to Senator Southard's report of February 2, 1835.

General Babcock's report to me is a tabular statement of the date of the acts of Congress, the amount of the appropriations, and for what purpose made. It is of too great length to embody in my remarks, but I will give the results. It covers expenditures on the Capitol grounds, at the President's House and grounds, the grounds of all the different Departments, and, in short, everything but the public buildings themselves. It includes the Mall and reservations generally, and the small triangular squares at street intersections, and also the salaries of officers, amounting to nearly $150,000.

With this explanation I will restate the account from the balance shown in second statement already given:

Grand total expended by District government for all purposes.....		$26, 295, 141 32
Total expended by the General Government, as shown in second statement, for municipal expenses, streets, &c..	$10, 841, 926 70	
Total expended by Government around public buildings, and on squares, parks, &c., to December 29, 1834.	49, 119 00	
Total expended on public grounds, parks Capitol and President's House, Smithsonian, and grounds around the Departments, as per General Babcock's report, since 1834..	1, 978, 318 09	
Grand total of Government expenditures............................		12, 869, 363 79
Difference between expenditures of the United States and the District of Columbia, in favor of latter..................................		13, 425, 777 53
Necessary to reimburse the District of Columbia, being one-half the difference..		6, 712, 888 76

I should observe that some items of the expenditures given by the Treasury Department as improvements of streets are also included in General Babcock's statement as improvements of squares, parks, &c., and really increase the credit side of the account of the Government; but I have not separated them, as it involved an examination of vouchers for which I had not the time to devote. The amount will not exceed $100,000 probably, and may fall below it. I must also observe that I have given the District government no credit for its expenditures on account of salaries of officers and employés other than those connected with the board of public works. Still, Mr. Chairman, it will be seen that, after allowing the United States credit for every cent it has expended which in the remotest degree has contributed to the joint benefit of the local and General Governments, we find the United States indebted to the District of Columbia in the sum of $6,712,888.76.

If I am right in my assumption, and I think that the closest calculation will not materially change it, that the United States should reimburse the District its excess of one-half the expenditures here for the common good, I am brought to the statement of the first duty of Congress, namely, to appropriate money sufficient to make this reimbursement.

If we were trying this case on a bill in equity, there would be a large item of interest properly chargeable to the United States on account of the advances made by the District government. There would also be another large item in the proceeds of sale of lots, and interest upon the amount. These, if considered, would more than double the balance which I have shown to be due.

But we seek to drive no hard bargain with the United States, and would not even ask reimbursement if we had a business interest, manufactures, trade, commerce, or revenues, to which we could look in the immediate or remote future for reimbursement.

But, sir, if we have any rights which can be enforced by an appeal to a sense of common justice, to a sense of national honor and fair dealing, I must believe that this first duty which I have pointed out will sooner or later be discharged.

Our statute-books are filled with precedents for reimbursements to the States upon precisely the same principle as that involved in this claim. I would not pretend to give the number of millions of dollars which have been appropriated by Congress to refund to States moneys which they had paid out for the common benefit of the whole people.

The second and imperative duty of Congress is to devise an intelligent apportionment of the expenditures at the seat of government.

It is not of half so much importance that large appropriations should occasionally be made, as that there should be a fixed and definite sum appropriated annually, which shall be disbursed with reference to an intelligent and wise development of the extraordinarily beautiful plan of our capital city. An appropriation annually by Government, which would not exceed five cents *per capita* of the whole population of the United States, together with local taxation, would sustain a fund sufficient in twenty years—yes, even in ten years—to make here a city unparalleled for its beauty.

There is no city in the Old World of which I have any knowledge that can compare for a moment with ours in the magnificence and grandeur of its plan. In all London there is not a street or avenue, after leaving the public parks, over which there is the least pleasure to drive. Almost the same thing may be said of Paris, with the exception of two or three boulevards and the Champs Elysées. Unter den Linden, of Berlin, is paved with Belgian pavement, with surface drainage through its gutters, a rough, unkempt, untidy, and disagreeable street, and one must go beyond the western gate for a pleasure drive. The Ring Strasse of Vienna is a broad macadam avenue encircling a busy hive of active industries, whose devotees are crossing and recrossing and traversing this busy thoroughfare, rendering a pleasure drive upon it next to impossible; and here, as in Berlin, for air and refreshing recreation, the inhabitants are driven beyond the confines of the city. So of Brussels; so of Munich; so of Rome; so of Naples, except, perhaps, a portion of Chiai; so of Florence, except its suburban drives.

But here, when the bordering grass of our broad avenues and streets shall have become a mat of green, and our many varieties of beautiful forest trees shall lift their heads aloft and throw their grateful shade over lawn and pavement, the beautiful vistas which will be opened up, the superb works of architecture, which in our public buildings surpass anything in the world of their kind, breaking in picturesque variety the view, with the lovely spring and autumn skies which overspread us for half the year, will make Washington City what its founders promised for it.

True the capital cities of the Old World have their splendid monuments and works of art, old and time-honored and splendid private mansions, that are a delight to behold; but seen, and known, and familiar with, one must go beyond all these for that rest and recreation which of all things, to the thoughtful, overtasked mind, is indispensable.

Monuments, statues, and works of art will come to us in time; they are the result of many years; they will add a charm to the capital; but whether we ever have these or not, nothing can prevent this city from being the most delightful on either continent, if Government will only extend to it that fostering care which its founders promised.

Your ten thousand, and rapidly increasing number, of overworked, brain-weary public servants will have only to step from their offices or their homes into the open street to be in the midst of repose and quiet, and in the grateful presence of lawn and forest. The wisdom of our patriot fathers, who secured our public servants from the close, hot, and feverish atmosphere of a crowded, dense city of strife and panic and money-getting, and placed them with quiet and rural surroundings, is being vindicated day by day, as the growing wants of Government invite here the best blood of the nation to assist in its management.

What even small appropriations will accomplish when regularly made is so favorably exemplified by the present engineer in charge of public buildings and grounds, that I point to his work as a complete demonstration of the wisdom of this course. He has made the desert smile and the waste places blossom, and yet his expenditure has not been felt. A similar policy pursued toward improvements outside the parks and reservations, added to local effort, will repay the outlay a thousand times.

Nothing can be more clear, upon even a cursory view of the local government and its relations to the parent Government, than that the United States have never acted upon any well-defined theory, or with any consistency or unity; that while it has been just—indeed, almost generous—in certain directions, it has been parsimonious and mean in others; that its policy has been fitful and vacillating and uncertain, and calculated to keep the citizens of the District government in the most deplorable and abject condition.

What is needed above all things here is a consistent, well-defined policy on the part of Congress in the support of this District government. I think the local government has the right to ask that a proper balance-sheet should be struck between the United States and the District of Columbia.

The United States should have credit for its expenditures on behalf of improvements in the District of Columbia, and generally its aid in maintaining the local government, excluding, of course, those appropriations which are made to all the Territories or States. The District government should have credit for all its expenditures of like character. The United States should then appropriate a sufficient sum to meet its just proportion of the difference in favor of the District of Columbia. And there should then be determined a fair and just proportion of future expenditures to be borne by the United States and by the District of Columbia.

I have no special theory or choice as to how this common fund—the appropriations made by Government, and the revenues derived by taxes upon the private property—shall be managed or disbursed.

I believe, however, that a more inexpensive form of local government can be devised than the present one; but as the property of

private citizens and the interest of private citizens are equally involved with those of the Government, I believe that in any form which may be finally adopted the people should have a just representation. I do not believe that the general principle which underlies our theory of government ought to be violated, because of any peculiar political relations which this District sustains to the General Government.

I believe the people here are as competent to determine what is to their interest as the people of any other community; and as our theory of government submits that question to a vote of the people in all communities, and has done so in this for seventy years, I cannot give my consent to see this principle violated.

The large interest of Government here I concede can have no other representation than that provided by Congress, and Congress must judge as to the best means for protecting its interests.

I shall quarrel over no form Congress may prescribe. Give us some guarantee that the Government will henceforth do its duty, and will lift some of the burdens under which we are groaning, and we will cheerfully trust the wisdom of Congress to provide a just government for the District. Our interests are common. We who have chosen this city for our homes will never be found wanting in devotion to it as the nation's capital. I point with pride to the efforts of our citizens in former years, and especially under the new government, as proof of what we shall always stand ready to do.

The monuments of this devotion are seen on every hand. Ingratitude, envy, and hate of the hour may blur the vision of some, and shut out all generous and patriotic emotions from the hearts of others, but the work of the last two years will vindicate itself; and the prominent persons in this era of Washington's regeneration will stand side by side in history with the founders of this noble city. No man must hope for justice in his day. This is the age of slander; and if it were not for the courageous souls scattered here and there in public life, we might surrender hope and succumb to the ghouls.

There is one brave man who has dared to lift up his voice out of the midst of clamor, and remind Congress of its duty. He did it under a sense of high official responsibility. He did it, too, not upon the recommendation of some head of Department, and upon second-hand evidence, but from actual observation of the progress of improvements here. I will venture to say that no one man in the District of Columbia, not even the governor himself, has been the daily witness of so much of the work in its detail as this man. Like his great prototype, Washington, who watched the unfolding of the plan of the city with the same keen interest that a botanist would the unfolding of a rare flower, or an artist the development of a great picture, President Grant has watched the rescue of the capital from national disgrace, and, unsolicited, his strong sense of justice plainly reminds you of a duty too long neglected.

Mr. Chairman, I began my remarks by reminding gentlemen of the paternal interest felt by President Washington in the future of this beautiful city, and the deep solicitude shared by his patriotic associates around him for its future prosperity. I showed how the seal of the nation's plighted faith was stamped thus early upon it. I may, I think, with becoming fitness conclude my remarks by quoting from President Grant's annual message to this Congress. He says:

Under the very efficient management of the governor and the board of public works of this District the city of Washington is rapidly assuming the appearance of a capital of which the nation may well be proud. From being a most unsightly place three years ago, disagreeable to pass through in summer in consequence of the dust arising from unpaved streets, and almost impassable in the winter from the mud, it is now one of the most sightly cities in the country, and can boast of being the best paved.

The work has been done systematically, the plans, grades, location of sewers, water and gas mains, being determined upon before the work was commenced, thus securing permanency when completed. I question whether so much has ever been accomplished before in any American city for the same expenditures.

The Government having large reservations in the city, and the nation at large having an interest in their capital, I recommend a liberal policy toward the District of Columbia, and that the Government should bear its just share of the expense of these improvement. Every citizen visiting the capital feels a pride in its growing beauty, and that he, too, is part owner in the investments made here.

Mr. Chairman and gentlemen of the committee, I have endeavored to do my duty by pointing out yours. I commit the subject to your earnest, intelligent, and patriotic consideration.

○

www.ingramcontent.com/pod-product-compliance
Lightning Source LLC
LaVergne TN
LVHW011133110826
845150LV00008B/2314
* 9 7 8 1 4 1 8 1 9 3 8 9 8 *